THE

BIG BOOK

OF

ESSENTIAL COMPUTER TIPS

AND

INSIDER SECRETS

© Copyright 2019
SERENDIPITOUS FINDS PULBLICATIONS

Written, Compiled and Edited

By

Steven Milbrandt

FOREWARD

This book is presented as a general reference guide. It is not intended to be too large or narrow in scope as this will limit its effectiveness. Every effort has been made to provide quality material and solutions to problems that both the everyday and power user face. These are ideas when implemented will make a difference immediately.

Perhaps there is a topic covered that is not relevant to you. That is alright. This book approaches these subjects in a user friendly and accessible way. Technology changes rapidly. That is part of what makes it interesting. Technology often challenges people. The manufactures and engineers that design this equipment understand it, but many casual and utilitarian minded people become frustrated when something does not work the way they expect that it should. Understanding happens by interacting, making mistakes along the way, and often, learning a better, more efficient approach.

Many people have different ideas about terms like "essential" but after using a computer for more than thirty years, the subjects contained in these pages are things that I wish I had a fuller knowledge of at the beginning. Some people regard computers and technology as boring and unexciting. If the subject holds little interest for some it is often because they have not discovered a way to integrate it into their lives in a fun or novel way.

This is not an all-encompassing compendium, but rather a book that tries to speak generally about a number of different and important topics and themes.

It talks about things like

- Proper computer practices
- How to improve the efficiency and stability of your computer
- Computer security including two factor authentication and password management

- How to save money when using the computer

- Open source software

- Operating system update methods

- Online purchases and promo codes

These are some of the things you will learn.

Although there are other books about these subjects; this book may be a starting point for you. Explore these subjects in greater depth. Search for creative ways to consider the topics in these pages. Think about how these subjects may apply to you. How you decide to be involved with technology is your choice.

DEDICATION

This book is dedicated to Judy Lekkis. Thank you, Judy for all your support and encouragement over the years.   You have always been there for me.   I want to share this document with the world in the hopes that people will learn from and be encouraged by it. Judy, you are a focused and determined person full of talent. Continue to try new things. Your smile brightens the day of others You make a difference in the world. Thanks for caring.

This book is also dedicated to Leo Laporte.   Technology pundit and computer advocate for many years, his TWiT Netcast Network, and "The Tech Guy", a nationally Syndicated radio show, a part of the Premiere Radio Network has inspired this author and thousands of others for many years. Thank you, Leo. You can learn more about Mr. Laporte by visiting

https://twit.tv

http://techguylabs.com/

https://leolaporte.com/

Thank you, Leo for making technology fun and accessible to everyone.

INTRODUCTION

The computer is a marvelous piece of technology but many of us do not understand it. For some, it is a mysterious box that they would rather not use. They choose instead to interact with paper and pencil. Others welcome such technology and interact with it on a daily basis. Whatever side of the debate you are on, this book will help you with practical information that you can put to use immediately. It is easy to dismiss such a simple claim but wait until you read a few pages before you pass judgment.

I wrote this book because I want people to understand that technology can be fun! Yes, it is sometimes complex, but when broken down into simple steps it becomes easier to manage. People learn in different ways. Some learn by doing. This is a practical "hands on" approach. Others take the time to carefully read all the information, think about it and approach things in a very methodical way. Whichever way you choose to learn or use this book, I hope that you will find it useful. You can always return to its pages when you want to remember something.

The Complexity of the computer and technology in general means that it is fluid, always changing and evolving. Along with updates to the operating system, applications, design and functionality, change is the watchword. To avoid frustration when unexpected problems occur, step back, take a break and look for alternative solutions. Chances are, they exist. The best place to begin anything is the beginning.

Microsoft Windows is the most prevalent operating system in use today. This book will answer questions with respect to it. Some topics are more generic and can apply to different operating systems and devices including portable and cloud based. When possible devices and specifics will be mentioned to maintain clarity and continuity.

The computer revolution really began with people like Steve jobs and Bill Gates who saw the potential of the computer when others did not. Some will argue that it goes back further to big main frames of the 1960s, with punch cards and complex code. Accessible computing began when hobbyists assembled kits in their basements. They soldered boards, attached and built the equipment they imagined. It is because of people like Bill Gates and Steve Jobs that paths were forged for future generations. The computer emerged as a productivity machine, entertainment box, and all-around household appliance that we know today. Love it or hate it, the computer is here to stay.

The people who learn to use it efficiently and master its hidden secrets will be happier than those who simply turn it into a simple word processing an input device. Many people give up too quickly and throw up their hands in frustration. It has been said then it takes 10,000 hours to master any skill. This book is meant to be a shortcut. It is a roadmap toward quicker understanding.

Thank you for purchasing this book and having faith in an unknown publisher. Thank you too for your patience and dedication to learning. Let's begin…

CHAPTER ONE

HARDWARE SPECIFIC TIPS

In writing this book, I wanted to include tips that I knew when I started using a computer. Many people do not know that there are many shortcuts that can make your life much easier. For example, do you know what the shortcut Control + C will do when entered on a computer keyboard? That shortcut will copy any highlighted text and place it in the notepad. Control+ V on the other hand, will paste any text that is copied to the notepad into the document at its current location.

Apple computers also have many shortcuts that are displayed prominently at the top in the menu section of most applications. It is prudent to look at the top down menus present in every program before you begin using it. Many shortcuts will be represented there.

Here are some keyboard shortcuts on the Apple Mac that will improve your productivity.[1]

Command + Tab -This command moves through open applications and documents

Shift + Control + Power – Puts all displays to sleep

Command + Bracket - Pressing command Post [moves you between folders

Command + Shift + 3 - Takes a screenshot of the computer's screen

These are just a few of the commands that you can use. These shortcuts will greatly improve your speed on the computer because a few keystrokes can take the place of longer commands. Similar types of commands exist for Windows too. I will not show you a list of window shortcuts in this book, but you can discover them[2]

It should be noted, that the windows key referenced by the word "Winkey" is not present on all keyboards, modern and recent keyboards will include it. One of the most common places to go on a Windows machine is the file explorer for example.

It is here that you will find a representation of the file structure present on your machine either created by you as you add and delete things like folders or created by the operating system itself in the course of the computers daily operation. Therefore, it is very useful to know the command" Windows Key + E"

As a result of your using the computer, you will no doubt discover new and fascinating ways to use keyboard shortcuts to your advantage. Not only will they save you keystrokes, but it will save you time so you can focus more on the task you are trying to complete. It would also be helpful to memorize important ones such as control + C and Control + V that you will use often whenever editing documents.

Using shortcuts often will make them become second nature to you and you will become more proficient and precise in your communications with others. We have learned the first insider secret … keyboard shortcuts. Let's move on to chapter 2 and continue our learning.

CHAPTER TWO:

THE MOST IMPORTANT THING YOU SHOULD DO ON YOUR

COMPUTER BEFORE ANYTHING ELSE!

There are many things you can do with the computer. That is why it has become an indispensable tool in our society. Many people do not place enough importance on two important aspects of computing -- computer security and backup. I will explore the basic aspects of the first element, computer security as it applies to passwords in this chapter.

It will probably come as no surprise to you that passwords are disliked by many people because they are inconvenient. One of the most common passwords is simply "12345" or "password". These passwords (if you want to call them passwords) should never be used, unless you want a surefire way to have your accounts compromised and your data held for ransom. "Ransomware attacks" get their name because data is scrambled and encrypted on a computer and the only way a user can get their data back, (and there's no guarantee of this) is to pay the attacker whatever ransom they demand before they will unlock it.

One of the best ways to guard against this is to use strong, long complicated passwords that cannot be guessed or cracked using what is called a "brute force attack". Often an attacker will use specialized software with dictionaries loaded in to them to decipher common passwords, poorly constructed passwords and passwords with repetitive phrases such as "monkey123" are easily compromised.

Often passwords will be placed in easily accessible areas such as a sticky note stuck to a monitor. This is easy for the user, but it is also easy for anyone who happens to be walking by and can easily glance at the password.

Another concern is that the more complex and harder to remember a password becomes, the less likely people will want to use it in their daily lives because if it's difficult for others to guess, it's hard for them to remember and use. So, what's the answer?

Password Managers

The simplest and most convenient answer is to use what is known as a 'password manager". The Password manager is simply a way to store complex, hard to remember passwords securely so that they are easily accessible to the user, but hard for others to guess, reverse engineer or use brute force techniques to determine.

Usually password managers store their information securely in what is called the "password vault". Using this technique, a person does not need to remember all their passwords, but only the password that opens their vault in the software. This software is usually browser based and "browser agnostic". This means that password managers can be used with all of the most popular browsers such as Google Chrome, Firefox, Microsoft Explorer and others. This is usually accomplished by installing a browser extension. A browser extension is simple to install in seconds and extends the capability of the browser. Be careful to only install browser extensions from known and trusted sources like Lastpass, however.

In this way, passwords can be made long strong and secure and they do not need to be remembered. When a person turns on the computer and starts up their browser of choice there password manager is automatically loaded, the user can log into it and the password manager will automatically fill in a password as it is needed by various forms and logins on the Internet.

These password managers are encrypted and often depending on the sophistication of user can be further secured with what is called two factor or second factor security to provide a double layer of encryption and peace of mind. Two factor encryption will be explored further in another chapter of this book. For now, let us discuss the basics of password managers.

Two of the most common password managers in use today are "Lastpass" available from www.lastpass.com and "1Password "available from www.1password.com. Both of these options operate in similar ways, but the important thing is to use one. There're many different password managers on the market available on the Internet.

It is important to look carefully before you ultimately decide which one is right for you. The two examples above are the most commonly used password managers use today. Experts have examined these two password managers – Lastpass and 1Password. And verified these companies claims through independent audit and review. Having a password manager is one way to be more secure in the face of ever-increasing worries about breaches and security compromises.

Although there are different versions of Lastpass, depending on your use case such as business or personal, its principle use remains the same. An individual user would simply sign up for an account at www.lastpass.com and create a password to their vault. This is like the password to a combination lock. Once the password to vault is decided, that user simply does 3 things:

1. Installs the associated browser extension (This is done automatically by the install)
2. Logs into Lastpass after choosing a Username and Master Password

3. Sets options within the program according to their preferences

That's it! From that point on Lastpass will offer to generate long strong and secure passwords, store them in your vault for you and automatically log you in when a password is requested by a website,

Whenever you come to the password field on a website or form Lastpass will automatically fill in details for you whenever you are logged into your Lastpass account. That way, when you turn on your computer enter your master password and you're off to the races. Simple, quick and secure.

Now let us look at another insider secret...

SECOND FACTOR AUTHENTICATION!

We will explore two-factor authentication in the next chapter

CHAPTER THREE

AUTHENTICATION

AUTHENTICATION

In another example of necessity coming up with a solution to a problem, authentication was developed as a means to determine whether you are who you say you are.

The dictionary definition of "authentication" is:

Noun

1. the process or action of proving or showing something to be true, genuine, or valid.

   "the prints will be stamped with his seal and accompanied by a letter of authentication"

   ○ COMPUTING

   the process or action of verifying the identity of a user or process.

   "user authentication for each device ensures that the individual using the device is recognized by the company"

(Source: www.google.com)

26

Authentication is "the process or action of verifying the identity of a user."

Authentication means that you must verify that you are who you say you are.
In these days of Internet breaches, verification and authentication by whatever means possible is becoming more and more important.

Second factor, also known as "two factor authentication", means that in addition to any password a second method of verification is used. This second factor is most often accomplished by means of the Short Message System (SMS) messaging also known as text messaging to send a text to the holder of a cell phone, and that text usually contains a verification code of five or six numbers.

Be mindful however, SMS for a second factor authentication is not always as secure as one would think because today cyber criminals are more and more resourceful. These people can easily clone a cell phone SIM (Subscriber Identification Module) card using what is called "social engineering". This usually involves tricking a customer service representative of a cell phone company into transferring the number from a particular SIM over to another one. This essentially copies the SIM card and its carrier information. In this way, the cyber-criminal would receive all texts that the individual actual owner of the cell phone would receive.

A better method of two-factor authentication is to download a free application from either the iPhone app store or the Google Play store such as the **Google authenticator** or the **Last Pass authenticator**. These applications generate random numbers that change every sixty seconds and therefore cannot be spoofed or obtained through social engineering. A bad actor such as the cyber-criminal would need both your phone and the authentication code in order to gain access to your account. Since they will not have access to your phone or the authentication codes you are much more secure. This extra security is less convenient than without it, however, it is a good compromise between convenience and security.

It is called two-factor because two things are involved in the verification process -- your password and the code. This is simple compared to other more complex verification schemes such as biometrics, voice or hand print authentication and similar technologies.

To sum it up, authentication is the process of verifying who or what something is. It makes you more secure and safer online. We have seen that verification through second factor through the use of ab application is the most secure way to verify who you are. The most common methods for authentication include:

Something you know – a password

Something you have –a code generation tool like an authentication app

A physical characteristic – like a handprint or a biometric scan

A more advanced form of authentication is something like a **Yubikey**. A Yubikey is a small physical dongle, similar in size to a USB Flash drive, it can be programmed to unlock secure accounts that you want to keep secure, particularly ones containing more sensitive information such as an email account. Earlier in this chapter, password managers were discussed such as Lastpass and you can use an authentication dongle such as a Yubikey to secure your password vault so that even if someone managed to acquire your master password they could not access your passwords without the Yubikey itself. You can find out more about security and the Yubikey at www.yubico.com

It is Important to note here that proper computer hygiene, that is, correct practices when it comes to computer security are essential in today's ever-changing technological climate. Recent breaches of the security of large corporations such as Equifax and Target are examples of why this is critical. Large corporations often do not take proper responsibility for their security failures and therefore it is our responsibility collectively as a society to be secure. Looking the other way or giving a corporation a slap on the wrist by government because of large funding by lobby groups does nothing except perpetuate the status quo.

The proliferation of "BIG DATA", as it is called, along with its models for collection and distribution means that the everyday public often has no idea of either who has their data or what is being done with it. Often, in reality, it is sold to advertisers who market their products much more efficiently. The advertiser's goal is to sell as much to as many as possible. This practice, while it makes shareholders happy is eroding our privacy a little bit at a time.

It is often said," if you are not doing anything wrong, you have nothing to worry about. "That is an over-simplification. Governments are made up of people and people make mistakes. It is possible that someone in authority will make a mistake with your data and compromise your security through no fault of your own. Each of us should be concerned about our privacy and personal security and here's why. The more of our data we hand over the less control that we have in our lives. We are implicitly giving control over to people who may not have our best interests in mind.

CHAPTER FOUR

FALSE POSITIVES

Have you ever been so sure of something just because it has always been a certain way that you blindly follow the same path? That is exactly what people do with respect to antivirus software. In the early days of computers, advice around protecting your hardware seemed much simpler. Many believed, according to the prevailing wisdom that after you install an antivirus onto your system that everything from that point forward would be fine. This partially held true because there were less malicious software, viruses and bad things to worry about online in the early days of the Internet.

Fast forward to today, roughly thirty years later, and there are many ways that an unsuspecting visitor to the "information superhighway", as it was once called, can encounter difficulties. Problems online can include everything from browser hijackers to "ransomware", Trojan horses, root kits, "crapware" and unauthorized access through social engineering. While it is beyond the scope of this book to go into each of these problems in detail, the viruses make up a very small part of the problems that are encountered on the Internet every day.

Why does the general public still believe that an antivirus program will solve all of their problems online? Some less sophisticated computer users routinely express surprise when their computer malfunctions and is sometimes unrecoverable without a fresh install of whatever operating system they are using. The routine hygiene of any computer, that is, "the steps any user must take daily to protect their hardware and the data it contains", begins with caution and vigilance. Usually it is the actions of you and I, that is, the user of the machine that causes the problems we encounter with our computers.

An antivirus is one small part of the care and maintenance of a computer. Windows, most certainly the most popular and prevalent operating system in use today does not require you to install an antivirus if you are running Windows 10 because

Microsoft has built that into its most recent OS. You simply need to make sure that it is enabled which it usually is by default.

It is far more important to be careful what you do online. This will prevent problems before they occur. Responsibility for our own online safety will be explored in greater detail later. Understand the problems that an antivirus can cause and simple ways to prevent them is part of what will be talked about here.

The majority of Windows users should be using Windows 10 but people running an old operating system because of compatibility with older software is one reason for not upgrading. This brings with it a different set of security problems. Whenever possible always upgrade, accept security patches the minute they are suggested, turn on "automatic updates" and make sure that programs you choose to install are the most current versions available.

If you do choose to install an antivirus, please make sure that you deactivate Microsoft Defender (The antivirus included with Windows 10) as they can try to compete with each other and result in problems for your system. Often uninstalling an antivirus cannot be accomplished by simply going to 'add or remove programs" or going to whatever variation of this exists for your version of Windows. You must look for in antivirus's specific uninstaller or removal tool released by the company that published the software or an uninstaller found within the program itself. Trying to find an uninstaller online can also be difficult unless you go directly to the company's website Downloading something by simply clicking a link in your list of Google displayed search results without verifying its source is not advised. This could allow "bad guys" access to your system or cause your computer to become infected which is what you are trying to avoid.

Computer insiders and experts generally agree that an antivirus has become an ineffective tool in computer security especially when used as the only line of defence. Preventing viruses from reaching you is a far better option. One of the ways you can do this is by watching where you go online, only downloading software from reputable sources, avoiding illegal downloads, avoiding clicking on indiscriminate links and being very cautious online in general.

While this chapter has focused on the antivirus, the complexity of many operating systems and hardware, often makes owning a computer seem like a full-time job. Our focus should be on simplicity whenever possible. The Chromebook may be the answer that you have been searching for without realizing it.

Many people who are using Windows 10 or a comparable system do not understand that, for what they do, such a general-purpose operating system is unnecessary. Retailers have for years oversold the public and have falsely represented what they "need".

Many people should consider a Chromebook for example because they are a much more secure type of computer than a Windows or Mac machine. First developed by Google, (now renamed Alphabet), the Chromebook is based on the ChromeOS. On a Chromebook, everything is accomplished through the browser. Functionality of this machine is increased by adding extensions found inside the Chrome web store. This is directly accessible from within the machine. If a user encounters a problem a simple button press or "Power Wash" as it is called will return the computer to its original factory state. It is precisely because a Chromebook is simpler by design and functionality that it shines as a computing device for many.

Now manufactured by many different companies such as Acer and HP, a basic Chromebook, brand new can be purchased for under $300. For what most people do including surfing the web, uploading pictures, listening to music, sending email and generally consuming content, the Chromebook is more than sufficient for their needs. If you are in the market for a

computer, consider a Chromebook

At this point, hopefully you can see how putting all your faith for

your computer's health and security on an antivirus program is

not only ineffective but extremely foolish. Now consider safer

Internet browsing and how avoiding one small thing can make a

HUGE difference.

Let's talk about ...

CHAPTER FIVE

SAFER WEB SURFING

Safer surfing online can mean many things but think for a moment of something very specific, hyperlinks and their prevalence online. Unscrupulous people can use such links to hide the true destination of a particular click.

The term "hyperlink" refers to "a link from a hypertext file or document to another location or file, typically activated by clicking on a highlighted word or image on the screen" (Reference: Google)

Simply clicking on a link without knowing where it goes can have disastrous consequences for and unsuspecting computer user. Sometimes, hovering the mouse over the link can reveal where it goes but often a inks true destination is hidden or disguised. It is therefore important not to click on any link in a post or email from a source you do not trust or can properly verify

.

When hovering over a hyper link, even if part of a trusted domain is visible, examine the end portion of the link for a further clue of its validity or falseness. For example: Examine this URL www.google.playstore-home.ru

It looks like the link will take you to the Google Play Store, however this URL is fabricated. The tail of the domain is "ru". This is the domain country code for the Soviet Union. The actual domain name for the U.S. Playstore is www.play.google.com A hyperlink can be named whatever its creator wants. A Microsoft.com hyperlink may simply have that label and could go somewhere totally different.

Another key point to remember is that recently many top-level domains or TLDs as they are called now can be many other things besides .com or .net. Today, domains can consist of (DOT) .info, (DOT) .me, (DOT). club and many other designations. This can make it confusing. Exactly what is a legitimate domain and what is not.

What is a domain?

"A domain, in the context of networking, refers to any group of users, workstations, devices, printers, computers and database servers that share different types of data via network resources. There are also many types of subdomains."

 (Source Technopedia.com)

A domain consists of three parts:

The part – Before the dots

       Between the dots

       After the dots

The part of the domain name before the dots is also referred to as a sub domain. Another distinction to make when referring to a subdomain is that there can be different parts within a given area of a domain.

A quick glance at a domain may not be enough to tell you about the contents of a particular website. This is another reason why you need to be careful where are you browse online.

It is a common practice and quickly becoming a requirement that a commerce related site be securely encrypted for the protection and security of its visitors. A secure website has an "s" after the http and before the written forms of the URL. An example of this would be https://wellsfargo.com

Look for the "s" at the beginning of a URL so you know any transaction that you complete on that site is concealed both in the transmission and the receiving of the information.

USING A VIRTUAL PRIVATE NETWORK

If you are accessing the Internet in a public place, consider using a virtual private network also known as a VPN. A VPN is like a private tunnel between your computer and the public Internet.

When you use a VPN, your traffic is private and is indecipherable to anyone trying to spy on it. People often use a VPN in areas where free speech is suppressed and contrary viewpoints to authoritarian or dictatorial rule is severely punished.

It should be noted that not all VPN's are equal. First, using a free VPN is definitely not recommended. Everything cost money and maintaining a VPN does too. If you are receiving a service for free, that means you are paying for it with your data possibly being sold to a third party or with ads or other compromises in such things as service or speed.

One of the most popular VPNs is called, Nord VPN and while it is excellent, there are other virtual private network companies that are equally good. When you go to purchase a VPN service it is important to look at all features and make sure they suit your needs. For a good starting point, just surf to www.nordvpn.com They offer a wide range of features and they do not keep their logs. This is important because if law-enforcement subpoena them in court, they will be unable to produce any of that information and your security is maintained.

It is clear that things are not always what they seem when it comes to links, pages and the dangers posed by surfing unprotected with open Wi-Fi. Someone sitting at a nearby table to you can easily examine Internet traffic if some of the steps outlined above are not implemented.

Ultimately, it is everyone's responsibility to ensure his or her own safety online. Being vigilant and careful is not always easy, but it is necessary. Once a person has been compromised, things like data loss and identity theft become real possibilities and correcting such severe problems can take months or years and be expensive

Having talked about better ways to stay safe online, we can examine better ways to share content and information so that you and the people you interact with can stay safer too.

Let's talk about ...

CHAPTER SIX

BETTER WAYS TO SHARE ONLINE

The Internet, especially the early Internet, brought with it a sense of community and connectedness not seen previously. Computer clubs and associations gave people a chance to interact with each other, relate stories, exchange ideas and come up with many solutions to everyday problems. People began trading computer programs to make their machines run better and expand their capabilities.

Some people wished to maintain tighter control over their intellectual property, and they sought to protect it by every available means. Others saw the opportunity to help and believed the information should be free and available to everyone. While protecting intellectual property is important, there should be a balance between control and accessibility, especially where the outcomes could benefit large numbers of people globally.

But how do you share safely? How do you send a picture, link, music or any number of other things safely?

The first thing is never ever sharing anything by email attachment. Email attachments are the number one vector of attack used by bad guys. Why is that? One reason is that sending out mass emails is cheap and simple. Email attachments create curiosity on the part of the receiver and they may open something that they should not.

Email attachments can often contain malicious code that can be activated once the user downloads them. Never assume an attachment is safe just because it looks like it comes from someone you know. Become a cynical skeptic when it comes to everything you do online. Make it clear to all your friends and associates that you prefer not receiving attachments, but if they must, notify you in advance by phone or other conventional means if they intend to send you one.

How do you avoid sending an email attachment entirely? Here are a few practical ways.

Create safe links using popular Storage and file sharing services like Dropbox, Google Drive and Microsoft's One Drive. These sites and services allow the user to create links to an item and share the link securely with another person. The file is stored securely in the cloud on that particular company's servers. This also means that users do not have to fill their email box with large files. It ensures that the recipient has the space or the bandwidth to download it properly. Also, if a person has a slow Internet connection, they will not appreciate you sending them a large file as an email attachment.

Use commercial file sharing services like Sharefile

"Many companies need to be concerned about sending personal information over the Internet. People like doctors and lawyers must adhere to strict government regulation with respect to this. Acts in the United States Congress such as the "Health Insurance Portability and Accountability Act" of 1996 also known as HIPAA "was created primarily to modernize the flow of healthcare information, stipulate how personally Identifiable Information maintained by the healthcare and healthcare insurance industries should be protected from fraud and theft, and address limitations on healthcare insurance coverage"[3]

(source: Wikipedia)

HIPAA compliant industries must take special precautions to ensure that information is correct and how it is secured and protected. These groups must make sure whatever means they use to share information, that information's security, storage and distribution complies with all regulations.

There are many companies that provide a means to share files that is HIPAA compliant. Sharefile by Cytrix is one of the most widely known. They allow users of their service to maintain control over the files they send, see when they are opened or downloaded and give them total transparency over the whole process. You can learn more by visiting www.sharefile.com

Use Firefox Send (https://send.firefox.com/) as another good solution for Sending files up to two gigabytes securely and for free is. This is a new service developed and maintained by the makers of the browser Firefox. The only requirement is that a user sign up for free account and the file size is limited to 2 GB fin total per file sent.

Create links from within social media -- the popularity of social media sites such as Facebook, Twitter and Instagram provide an easy means for creating links from within the services in the shared files, photos and sound clips. These services provide a place where people with like-minded interests can "hang" out and share things of interest to them.

Previous information with respect to security must also be considered when using social media. Online security concerns must be at the forefront of any posting strategy. Large companies like Facebook have a history of abusing people's trust and result in security breaches

(-- Examples of which are the" Cambridge Analytica scandal" and the compromise of user data and passwords) means that in shared on these services should not be considered guaranteed secure. Many companies have a habit of asking for forgiveness and not asking for permission.

Safer sharing is possible if you use one of the methods outlined above. Maintaining an understanding of company policy with respect to privacy and changes in terms and condition is our responsibility and when in doubt, ask.

CHAPTER SIX

SPRING CLEANING

There is often much talk about how to increase a computer's performance. Since the computer became mainstream in the early 1980's, consideration has been given to many different components that are factors in a computer's performance such as more RAM, CPU, a faster graphics card and other things. Often, very little attention is afforded one of the most basic of tasks that can dramatically improve the performance of a computer system -- erasing the computer's hard drive and starting over. That may seem like an extreme oversimplification to say that performing this very simple task will dramatically improve everything going forward.

It would be right to suggest that such a task might be time-consuming. It is true reloading the operating system from scratch has traditionally taken a significant amount of time but now that has changed. There are shortcuts you can take to reduce that time such as finding more efficient ways, to automate some of the job. In this way, something that may have felt intimidating to you in the past, is not so hard. It is easier

57

when you know about more efficient methods. You might even come away smiling.

If you followed advice from earlier in this book and have begun to back up your data fairly frequently, there are steps that you can take to minimize the amount of time that a fresh install of Windows or any other operating system will take to get back in place and running the way you want.

Many people think that a backup properly done means backing up everything on the computer -- a bit by bit, sector by sector copy of the computer's hard drive. That is a full backup, however, as suggested earlier, the most important parts of any backup are that data, which is self-created and cannot be easily duplicated. That data properly backed up to external sources such as hard drives, USB flash drives or even conventional media such as writable CDs and DVDs and online with services serves like iDrive, Carbonite or Dropbox means that a restore becomes much easier.

Another thing that you can do to reduce the amount of time any future restore takes is to make use of what is called disk imaging. Disk imaging is the process of making a full copy of your hard drive when you have it set up correctly before you add and modify things that would ultimately slow down your system. This copy which can be made using easily available software. It is set aside for a future time when a full restore is necessary. Some of these programs are more complex than others but most automate the backup process so you can "set it and forget it", that is. walk away for the few hours it might take to complete. Later in this chapter this will be discussed in more detail following the eraser and restoration process.

When beginning to backup your computer, have certain things handy. (This includes your install authorization codes, activation emails, and passwords for newer software available) when you begin to reinstall your programs. There are nifty little reinstalling bundles that you can download. All of these batch (mass install) programs come preconfigured with many of the software programs that you use every day. In this way, you can choose the programs you want to install, and they are all installed with one click.

Prior to installing anything, start by erasing the hard drive. To a person new to computers, this may seem like an unnecessarily scary task, however with the right program, in a few easy steps you will wonder what you were ever frightened about. Remember, with backups already made, there is no need to fear.

One final mention must be made concerning older versus newer versions of Windows. The explanations that are provided in this book assume that you are using the newest version of Windows, that is, Windows 10. Under this latest version of Windows, serial activation codes (code separated by dashes required by the validation process in every version of Windows prior to Windows 10), is no longer necessary. When Windows 10 is purchased, installed and properly validated, the machine recognizes the install even if the hard drive is erased. Microsoft calls this process "entitlement".

If you are using an older version of Windows (anything prior to windows 10) most often Windows 7, a legally purchased copy of the software along with the 25-digit activation also called the serial number is necessary before the new install can be properly activated with Microsoft servers. Therefore, be sure to have that available before you erase your hard drive.

Many older computers include a hidden install or recovery partition on the hard drive. This provides a way, (usually when you do an upgrade in place from within Windows itself) for the install procedure to use that hidden partition and get the user up and running quickly. So if you have an older computer running an older version of Windows, doing a simple Google search for whatever manufacturer and model number plus the words "restore procedure" will provide you with the series of key commands required to activate this, provided of course, the manufacturer included a restore partition.

For example, to access the hidden recovery partition on an older Dell XPS Studio laptop you would:

Restart the computer and press the "F8" key repeatedly after the Dell logo appears on the screen until the Advanced Boot Options menu appears. Select "Repair Your Computer" and then click "Enter." Enter the administrator's username and password associated with the computer, and then click "Enter" again.

However, this procedure varies by manufacturer and model number. Consult the documentation that came with your computer or the manufacturer's support website.

The first step is erasing the hard drive. There are two main types of hard drives on modern computers a spinning drive and a solid state or SSD. Spinning drives contain platters, a read/write head and moving parts and are therefore, easier to erase. As more and more people are purchasing computers with solid-state drives (SSDs), beginning there is a logical choice.

Erasing solid-state drives cannot be accomplished using tools like "Darik's Boot and Nuke" – a common hard drive eraser software tool (DBAN) because of the different way that things are stored on those types of drives. There are many tools available one of them is called, "Parted Magic". This is a free piece of software that allows you to easily erase solid-state drives with a few steps. I am going to outline them here briefly.

Download and install "Parted Magic" on a USB flash drive. This is a free open-source program from a well-respected software distributor called "Source Forge" https://sourceforge.net/projects/partedmagic/

Next you must download and install another utility called "UnNetBootin" you can find the "UnNetBootin" utility at this webpage https://unetbootin.github.io/

this utility allows for the creation of a bootable USB flash drive. After creating this drive and put the "Parted Magic" program on it, we can use Parted Magic" to securely erase any SSD drive. For a full explanation of all the steps involved you can visit [4]

A conventional spinning drive can be a race more easily using a program called, Darik's Boot and Nuke" this program is also free and can be found at https://sourceforge.net/projects/dban/ Neither "Parted Magic" or "Darik's Boot and Nuke" are too complicated to use, but they do require that you follow specific steps to achieve erasure of either a solid-state drive or conventional spinning drive. A detailed explanation of installing and using "Darik's Boot and Nuke" is present in a great deal of detail at a well-known tech blog called "Lifewere"[5] Erasing a hard drive, whether it's a solid-state drive or conventional spinning drive is a good way to improve performance on a computer because over time debris from installing and deleting various programs is left behind on the hard drive and this can cause problems such as performance lag and other issues. It may seem like a drastic step to erase a hard drive like this but performing such a step every 24 to 36 months is a good way to ensure peak performance.

You may not want to erase your hard drive because you think this involves a great deal of work and many hours. Shortcuts such as batch install programs can install commonly used software fast. In this way, it can dramatically reduce the amount of time it takes to get your computer back up to the state it was before you erased the drive. Another important thing to remember is that if you follow the backup steps outlined earlier in this book, your data is already backed up so after you batch install frequently used programs, you can recover your system to its original condition quickly. Now it will be operating much quicker because of the fresh start on a clean drive.

Now let's talk about another way to dramatically increase the way to recover from a problem with the computer let's discover...

CHAPTER SEVEN

PERFORMING A CLEAN INSTALL OF WINDOWS

Performing a clean install of Windows used to be a long and rather arduous process. Today, thanks to improvements to the operating system and Windows 10 it is fairly simple and straightforward. Now that you have successfully erased either a solid-state drive or an optical spinning drive, it is time to begin the process of reinstalling Windows.

Please note that there will be slight variations for how to complete this procedure for older operating systems of Windows such as Windows 7. Uses if Windows operating systems older than seven are not occurring as frequently. It is also important that anyone who is using Windows 7 currently will be doing so without any updates after January 14, 2020. This is the date Microsoft ends extended support for Windows 7.

This means that although you can continue to use Windows 7 after that date there will be no further security updates a or patches unless you are corporation opted for continued support under a separate multi license agreement. [6]

You have a few options for performing a clean install of Windows. The first is to create a Windows installation USB flash drive using the Microsoft Windows media creation tool. You can find the Windows media creation tool at

https://www.microsoft.com/software-download/windows10

Before you begin this process, it is important to have a new or newly erased USB stick that you can use to put the Windows 10 software onto. This typically requires a USB flash drive of at least 16 MB. Once you download the creation tool from Microsoft, it is a fairly simple process to follow the steps the software defines to create installation media. It should be noted however that you should only get this tool from Microsoft in order to avoid the danger of malicious software from unknown sources. Go back to the previous chapter in this book if you need a reminder of how to prepare your drive for installation.

As stated previously, it is important to have all your files backed up so that you can easily restore them on your clean drive. The 1-2-3 backup strategy, that is, one local backup a second copy off-site in the third copy on a cloud backup service. Cloud backup service is another word for off-site. Usually this involves a commercial program that the company backs up on their servers. (Examples of cloud backup services include Carbonite, iDrive or Backblaze)

Of all the consumer grade backup services, I like Carbonite and idrive respectively. Idrive allows you to backup all your devices for one low price. The first year of idrive service is usually subsidized because the company uses this as an incentive to promote new subscriptions. Being able to backup an unlimited number of computers, tablets, cell phones or whatever else is available in your network for one low price is very attractive. The first year is usually 90% off, so the service costs typically around $29. Depending on the plan you choose the second year can be double that. The company usually gives you approximately a terabyte of space and you can upgrade to more if you find that's not enough.

Idrive and the other services also generally provide a means to backup that will speed up the process such as sending you a hard drive that you can connect to your system and then return it to them. This way you can speed up the backup process. Off-site backups that use your own bandwidth are often very slow because they depend upon your upload speed. Even if you download speed is fast, your upload speed is the most important aspect to consider when talking about the time off-site backup requires.

The second option to perform a clean install of Windows is to do a reset. There are reset settings in Windows 10 which will roll it back quickly. To do this all you have to do is open up the settings tab, select update, then select the security option and finally select recovery.

To recap then:

- We have discovered how to use the program Parted Magic to securely erase solid state hard drives
- We Demonstrated how to use the DBAN program to erase spinning hard rives

- We have demonstrated how you can perform a clean install of Windows

A clean install of Windows is good to perform what's every 18 to 24 months. Starting fresh means that any of the slowdowns created by things such as garbage left from deleted programs such as dynamic link files (.dll), cruft and unnecessary elements of programs and files that are the result of installing and deleting programs over time. This occurs as a result of no fault of the user. Over time the computer may simply appear sluggish.

A clean install also has the added benefit of getting rid of any malware, viruses, or problems that you did not even realize that you had on your system. Most people think viruses, root kits or malware in general, want to be found. Unless it is ransomware designed for the purpose of getting you to perform an action like paying for the removal of a virus or ransom, most of these nefarious tools do not want to be found. They prefer to operate in the background without the user's knowledge or permission.

This way they can compromise systems for use as " botnets", D-

DOS (Denial of Service attacks) and other bad things.

CHAPTER EIGHT

THE POWER OF DRIVE IMAGING

Earlier disk imaging was mentioned as a way to dramatically increase the speed at which you can go from System failure to complete restore in a matter of minutes. Network administrators and system pros use this strategy often. In a Business environment, downtime costs money and productivity. Previously, we discussed how batch-installing applications makes reinstalling simple and quick. Network administrators do this all the time using large-scale deployment strategies of updates and patches over a network among standardized machines and equipment.

As a home user, you can use similar strategies through disk imaging. Disk imaging software makes a complete copy of entire target hard drive that can be used to restore a system quickly. Disk imaging programs are freely available for download that do this job well and for very low cost.

Disk imaging is a very powerful tool that anyone has at his or her disposal to quickly and easily be up and running again in minutes not hours or days. We will see how practical such a strategy can be when properly implemented. Some home networks today have four; five, six or more Systems to maintain.   Perhaps in a large or small business any number of computer systems might be set up.   Having the ability to quickly restore a computer from a disk image makes absolute sense.

Drive imaging is like making a freeze-dried copy of every bit on your hard drive. This is very useful because after you make a full disk copy, it is easy to reload it with a single click. Drive imaging means that after you get your hard drive erased and restored to exactly the way you want it some of the techniques described in this book, you can make a drive image copy. That way, the next time there is a problem with your computer or it crashes, you can easily restore it with drive images backed up previously.

Some Drive imaging programs are more complicated than others

- Clonezilla   http://clonezilla.org/
- EaseUS   http://www.easeus.com/
- Drive Snapshot http://www.drivesnapshot.de/
- Macrium   http://www.macrium.com/
- DriveImageXML   http://www.runtime.org/

These programs all do a similar job, but it is up to the user to discover which ones they prefer. Ease US is a free and easy to use program that many people use to successfully backup and create a drive image that is easily restored when necessary. It is important to note that documentation will also vary depending on the use of the software and the detail they provide

Having a good drive back up and running quickly so that you can complete the tasks of your day is essential. This is important because, as discussed previously, it can never be known with certainty when a problem with the computer will occur. Being ready at any time means having a good backup strategy and incorporating disk imaging into it.

As with any new program, it will take a while to become proficient with whatever disk imaging program that you choose.

Do not get discouraged. With repeated use and careful study all of these things will become second nature to you. Drive imaging is not particularly well known among the general public, but it is widely practiced by businesses because they want to be sure and get their systems up and running quickly. Network operators use this method to get some of their systems working after a Microsoft windows upgrade. They will create one media that contains all the patches and upgrades in one convenient package and dispatch that to all the systems on their network. This type of batch installation ensures uniformity, speed and productivity is maximized.

CHAPTER NINE

HOW TO REINSTALL YOUR FAVORITE PROGRAMS WITH

LIGHTNING SPEED

GETTING YOUR PROGRAMS AND SYSTEM BACK QUICKLY

Now that you have the operating system back on your computer, we can get your programs back quickly with simple shortcuts. There're many programs that can be bulk or batch install with one click. These are basically packaged collections of applications. This means that once you download the batch installer that has the programs you want to install; you simply check off / choose the applications that you want installed. The installer will automate the process. Once initiated, most of these installers can operate unattended until finished This really makes installing programs quick and easy. Just choose the installer that best meets your needs let the program do the rest

Batch installers as they are called are collections of computer programs. To use any of them you simply check off the programs that you want to install in one group and the installer will do the rest. One of these well-known installers called "NINITE". Additionally, there is also "NPACKD', "ALLMYAPPS' and "SPEEDINSTALL".

All of these batch installers essentially do the same thing, install a bunch of programs at once. Many of these can be set so that you can turn it on and forget it. These automated install features make it extremely easy to just start the program and walk away. you can learn more about all of these programs what they do and where to find them[1] at https://www.hongkiat.com/blog/batch-install-uninstall-windows/

---

[1] Source : https://www.hongkiat.com/blog/batch-install-uninstall-windows/

Now is the time to...

INSTALL THE REMAINDER OF YOUR SOFTWARE COLLECTION

Gather together the remainder of your favorite programs. You might also consider whether you really need any given program. Every program that you install includes with it the possibility of errors in the program code, potentially exposing you to an undiscovered vulnerability that could lead a bad guy to find new ways of causing problems for you – the unsuspecting user.

It is good practice, to reduce the possibility of the problems or risk whenever possible. Limiting what you install on your machine is one way to do this. It also forces you to be more selective in what you choose to install, how you choose to interact with those programs and, such a strategy, means that you will only install what you use most often. Choice like that has the added benefit of streamlining your reinstallation process. This means that in the future clean installs will happen even faster.

SOME FINAL THOUGHTS ABOUT IMPROVING SYSTEM PERFORMANCE AND OTHER NECESSARY TASKS

Much has been covered in this chapter and in this book as a whole to jam pack it full of amazing content so you will know what computer professionals do to stay one step ahead and Keep their systems running optimally. A summary of what has been included follows:

- ✓ You learned about optimizing computer Performance by performing scheduled backups

- ✓ You learned about speeding up the computers performance by performing a clean install every two years

- ✓ You learned about the tools such as "Derik's Boot and Nuke" and "Parted Magic"

- ✓ You learned about disk imaging and its power

- ✓ Discovered Batch installation of programs and

services

✓ You learned about being judicious about what you

choose to install

Now what one final element puts all this together into one

unifying whole?

CHAPTER TEN

"PROPER COMPUTER HYGIENE"

Proper computer hygiene, that is, wise computer practices that should be followed to maintain the health and security of any computer system. These practices are not as important on air-gapped equipment (equipment not connected to the Internet). A good rule is to always practice them whether air gapped or not. This ensures protection always.

Standards must always include:

- ✓ Accepting all operating system security patches and any update as recommended by the manufacturer such as Microsoft
- ✓ Not obtaining software from questionable vendors
- ✓ Backup the computer regularly
- ✓ Be sure to include self-created files that cannot be easily duplicated if lost
- ✓ A proper backup strategy requires thought and effort.
- ✓ If something is not easy most people will not do it.. (Therefore, simplify your backup strategy with cloud

backup solutions such as iDrive, Carbonite or Backblaze

(detailed in an earlier section of this book)

Most people do not think about data loss until it happens to them. Personal data loss is one thing, but company data loss can have catastrophic effects on a company and can often lead to its eventual demise.

In today's world of data breaches, accidental losses, natural disasters and other calamities, maintaining our data is hard work. Usually large corporations have entire teams tasked with maintaining the safety and security of their critical infrastructure. Whatever the situation, a backup strategy is always important

BACKUP REGULARLY, OFTEN AND AUTOMATICALLY

A popular backup strategy called "3-2-1 Backup refers to the way a backup is implemented. A "3-2-1 Backup" refers to having three copies of any file in two places and one backed up offsite. This strategy ensures that data loss is minimized It should also be noted that one copy of anything is not a backup.

There are as many ways to backup as there are opinions about it. You could backup on a USB thumb drive, a portable connected hard drive, a multi-drive network attached storage device (NAS) or an offsite climate control server such as Amazon Web Services (AWS) or use a file sharing service such as Dropbox

Whatever solution you choose, back things up often and on a regular schedule.

As mentioned in the "3-2-1 Backup Strategy" offsite backup is a critical component. If there is a fire, flood or other disaster where your backups are stored, those backups, while good, will not survive. Popular off-site backup solutions include companies like iDrive, Carbonite and Backblaze. Each of these solutions has positive and negative components attached to them. It is important to do your research before making your final choice.

- ✓ Considerations such as:
- ✓ How many computers can be backed up with a single Account?
- ✓ How file versioning is handled?
- ✓ Are there additional costs for attached storage devices such as external hard drives?

iDrive for instance, allows a user to back up to as many devices as they want on one account.

Most services such as iDrive are based upon a subscription model that renews yearly. An important thing to remember with these services is that online backup is only as fast as the upload speed provided by your Internet service provider (ISP). Most ISP's emphasize their download speeds, but with online backup services like iDrive, upload speed is the most important factor for consideration.   Many companies will quote a download speed in excess of 75 GB or higher per second while disclosing the upload speed of 5 gigs or less with an asterisk at the footer of their sales copy.   Online backup because of bandwidth limitations is a slow process As mentioned earlier, many companies like iDrive will send you a hard drive upon request that you send back to them with your files copied directly to it that making the process of backup much faster.

CHAPTER ELEVEN

PHOTO STORAGE TIPS

Not very many years ago in the age of film, when people thought about photography it was usually print photography. You would go to the camera shop and purchase rolls of 24 exposures (print) film, put it in your camera and set out on your quest for your perfect shot. After completing the role, you would need to wait at least an hour or possibly a day until the pictures were developed. When the digital camera made its appearance in the 1980s, everything changed!

The digital camera makes it easier for anyone to take pictures, see the results instantly on an electronic screen and decide immediately if they want to keep the picture. The ease-of-use and immediacy of results has made many people "snap happy". The cost of taking pictures has dropped dramatically since the popularity of digital cameras.

Also changed, is the resolution of the pictures these cameras are capable of capturing. Two-megapixel cameras once considered top-of-the-line have now been relegated to the back of the closet. The industry responded and manufactures are turning out cameras capable of many times that resolution and optical zoom standard. Even more interesting is that since the smartphone took off beginning in 2007 when Apple's iPhone changed everything (both in terms of compactness and feature richness), the iPhone meant that most smart phones that followed also included a decent camera.

The hundreds of pictures taken every day by people all around the world brings new challenges for everyone taking those pictures – where to put them? Sometimes people just leave them on their portable devices – their phones, tablets and the camera's SD card. The problem is that when their devices fail, those people run the risk of losing their precious memories.

There are much better ways to keep your pictures, so they are freely available for you anytime, anywhere. Many of these solutions are free or very low-cost.

The best option for most people right now is available from Alphabet Incorporated. Alphabet is the parent company of Google and Google provides a number of services that are excellent for the average user. One of these is "Google Photos". Accessible online with the simple URL www.photos.google.com Google provides users with the means to safely and securely store all the digital photos on Google servers for free. This also means that as photos are uploaded to Google, people can, if they choose, erase them off of their device and save space. In this way anyone can put any number of photographs on the Google cloud for no cost.

The process of storing photographs on Google is simple. The person simply downloads the Google Photos application from the Apple App Store or the Google Play store, tweaks a few settings allowing Google to upload the photos from their phone or other device. When those pictures are safely on Google servers there is an option to delete them from your device. This does not mean that they are gone forever from your phone or other device. You can download them again at any time. This increases storage room on your device for other photos or applications. There is a paid tier for the service. If you want original full quality, you can pay Google a small monthly fee. However, if you allow Google to store all your photos slightly compressed, there is no cost.

Allowing Google to store your photos makes practical sense. They are safe from accidental deletion, loss caused by hardware malfunction and from the disasters which might happen with print photographs at home. Google provides this free service in exchange for being able to use this data to help improve its machine learning engine which includes its facial recognition technology.

Discounting the fears of some people concerning Google having access to their images, it has been said that of the big five technology companies, it comes down to who you trust the most with respect to your data. Since Google provides their photo storage service at no cost unless you choose to upgrade. This is a very attractive solution to the problem of photo storage.

Apple is a good choice because they have shown themselves to be a leader with respect to customer privacy. Their business is not in selling customer data like Google or Facebook. However, portable storage with Apple costs more. Apple only gives you 5 GB of storage for free and after that they charge a monthly fee. However, for some people entrenched in the Apple ecosystem, Apple provides a good choice because they don't have to think about anything extra outside of Apple and iCloud with iPhoto storage integrates very well with all their devices including the iPad, iPhone and the Apple watch.

Google and Apple are not the only storage options for your photographs. For Amazon prime subscribers, free photo storage is included with their yearly or monthly membership fee. Storage on Amazon's servers Amazon Web Services (AWS) also provides a safe and secure place for your memories.

Microsoft has the One Drive Storage. They also offer generous allowances of free space for photographs or other types of data files on their servers. Microsoft's previous business model consisted almost entirely of generating revenue from its Windows operating systems, has become very diversified in recent years. Once extremely proprietary in nature, it has worked to include cell phone-based apps on many platforms lately.

For many people, Dropbox (www.dropbx.com) is a good solution because of their file sharing options. Download the Dropbox app on all your devices where you want your files. The application places a special "Dropbox" folder on every device that it is installed on. Just drop any file that you want to share with any of your connected devices This designated Dropbox folder images instantly available on each of those devices.

There are also specialized services -- some cost money and others offer free features. For those looking for other options, these are worth consideration.

A few of these are:

Flickr (www.flickr.com)

Smugmug (www.smugmug.com)

Adobe Creative Cloud (www.adobe.com/crativecloud/)

Wherever you choose to keep your photographs, the solution and choice is a very personal one and it is specific to the user and their use cases. Perhaps you are a leadite. The Urban Dictionary (www.urbandictionary.com) defines a leadite as:

"a term used for those who are afraid of computers, the Internet and the digital age. They prefer to stick to pencil (lead) and paper. It is a modern variant of the term Luddite. That old timer doesn't believe in using computers. That leadite prefers to write everything down with pencil and paper."

If you call yourself a leadite, you store your photographs – the tangible kind printed on photo paper in a cool, dry place that is properly ventilated and free from humidity and other forms of moisture.

CHAPTER TWELVE
COUPON
CLIPPER

Most people want to save money. Costs of goods and services seems constantly on the rise. What was $5 a short time ago creeps up to $5.25, $5.45 or $5.79 before you realize it. Inflation and misleading package sizes or quantities also means everyone wants to save whenever they can

People still clip coupons from print media. North American shoppers make it a daily ritual to look to their flyers and cut out paper coupons. There are many apps available for these buy smartphone phone that make this process digital such as FLIPP. Looking at the small screen is not always pleasant and can result in eyestrain and delays at supermarket checkouts.

There are other ways to save money online that you may not have heard about. Online coupons also called promotional codes or promo codes can save you a lot of money, but it is not always obvious where to find them and might not be offered by the retailer or vendor where you shop.

Today online shopping makes up a large percentage of all the goods bought and sold, and in many cases, the physical "brick-and-mortar" stores are declining at least in some sectors of the economy for specific types of purchases. Some items need to be tried on to make sure of their proper fit, size and style for the person's individual tastes. Digital downloads can involve the selling of information. Items bought online, can, in many cases, be downloaded instantly with no waiting. This satisfies our appetite for instant gratification and immediate consumption. You could be losing out on hundreds of dollars each year by not using promo codes.

Promo codes can be advertised or tacked on the end of a URL such as www.curbsidebooks.com/save25 (only an example) but other codes must be hunted down like a bird searching for its prey. Let us discuss some places where promo codes can often be found and what to do when you find them.

Here are a couple examples of coupon code sites

RetailMeNot www.retailMeNot.com

Honey Coupons   www.joinhoney.com

"RetailMeNot" allows users to go to their website and search for available coupons for the product or service they are interested in purchasing online.   Sometimes, this is an exercise in patience because it takes a few tries to find one that works. If you do a Google search in the form:

PRODUCT + PROMO CODE

Once found, you just copy and paste these codes into a promo box somewhere around the vendors website and receive the discount at checkout.   Some codes are valid while others have expired and the user must try a few before they receive a discount, usually seen by an immediate decrease off the original price.

Honey (www.joinhoney.com) is different because to it you can join honey as a member and install the browser extension. When you visit a website, Honey searches online for the best available discount and fills it in automatically for you.

Finding and implementing coupon codes or promo codes may seem like a lot of work at first glance, but you can save 40, 50 and 60 percent off the list price in many cases. In cases where what you are buying is a monthly subscription, a promo code becomes even more important because the savings extend monthly until you cancel.

Sometimes, promo codes are made available exclusively to company newsletter subscribers. Often these deals are like flash sales and expire in a day or even a couple of hours. These newsletter promo codes are to get people reading their newsletters and engaging them. People become engaged and happy customers who will keep coming back and return for future opportunities even if they are not interested in the present offer.

The lesson here is to be open to every possibility to save money whenever and wherever you can.

Here are a few things to remember:

- ✓ Look for new websites – often these offer specials to attract new customers
- ✓ Sign up for email newsletters but use a special email address just for marketing mail so your regular inbox does not become flooded with messages
- ✓ Use money-saving smart phone applications like FLIPP
- ✓ Look for promo codes when you are looking to make a specific purchase online.

CHAPTER THIRTEEN

OPEN SOURCE SOFWARE

In the context of saving money, you may or may not have heard the term "open source". Open source is a broad term that relates to the idea that computer code should be shared and made available to others. This belief is in contrast to the proprietary business model of most companies or organizations where profit is the primary goal or motivation for creating of product

The Website http://www.opensource.org goes into detail about this. They say:

The term "open source" refers to something people can modify and share because its design is publicly accessible. Open-source software is amazing. First, there is a great variety available and it covers a wide range of topics and interests. Open-source does not necessarily mean free, but in many cases it is. Often, open source is the first place I look for quality software to do a specific task. The community-based atmosphere around the open source community means that people are proud of what they design and want to share it with the world.

This is opposite the business model which is clearly motivated by profit. The open source community loves to share and wants to make a difference in the world around then. It is not always free because like everything else in the world, software development cost money and so does the education that developers needed to produce the talent they have.

If you think about it, most people want to make a living. The open source community needs either a source of revenue or people willing to donate so they can keep developing what they love and help others at the same time. Open source projects, products or initiatives embrace and celebrate principles of open exchange, collaborative participation, rapid prototyping, transparency, meritocracy, and community-oriented development.[2]

Open source software should matter to everyone because its model is different. Open and freely accessible means better

---

[2] To learn more about the opensource community and concept, you cab visit http://www.opensource.com

security. If the source code can be examined, back doors can be found, and security holes patched. It is harder to conceal back doors or a secret way into a program if that program is open and freely available for inspection by everyone who cares to look.

The collaborative and cooperative nature of open source means people are working together, sharing and finding solutions to common problems and difficulties that they may face while using the open-source software. Often users and developers are very passionate about what they produce. It is nice to have someone to help if anyone has a question or concern.

Linux for example, is an open and freely available operating system that is not only free to download and experiment with its code, but there are many types or distros of Linux the hobbyist or tinkerer can always try a new version. If they do not like it, they can delete it and try another. This means that instead of being limited to proprietary business for profit software, you could save a lot of money provided you are willing to experiment and learn new things.

Trying Linux is not for the "out-of-the-box "mainstream user who is use to Windows or Apple's Mac OS because some commercial programs do not have an open source equivalent, but more and more applications are being developed so there is less and less of the divide or lack. Indeed, for the open-minded user who is willing to learn, there are often more choices not less. There are also many forums where users can learn and exchange ideas. Open-source users are proud of the community they belong to online and cannot wait to shout their enthusiasm from the rooftops.

A quick Google search using terms such as "Best Linux for Beginners" will bring many results that you can try. You can also search http://distrowatch.com and take a look.

OPEN SOURCE SOFTWARE IS OFTEN FREE

For those on a budget, it is also valuable to know that most open software is free

If you are looking for a particular program to do something just search

Program type + open Source

For example –

- ✓ open source photo editor
- ✓ open source music player
- ✓ open source drawing program
- ✓ open source spread sheet

You get the idea …

If you do not like or want to pay a monthly or yearly fee to use Microsoft Office for instance, you can go to www.openoffice.org and download a full suite of office productivity tools, the equivalent of Microsoft Office for free.   You can even open a Microsoft Word file from within Open Office's Writer program.

There are many free and ultra-low-cost options available to you online if you are willing to take the time and effort to look. A word of caution, -- always look for reviews about whatever you are thinking of downloading so you can see what other people think before you install it.

Here are a few things to keep in mind when searching online for software:

- ✓ Always search for the software publisher's website so you can make sure you get it from a reliable source
- ✓ Look for reviews and opinions online before you download anything
- ✓ Be careful when installing software because sometimes install forms check boxes by default that you may not want
- ✓ if you don't like it, delete it immediately. Don't leave it there to clutter up your system and potentially cause you problems

- ✓ If you are unsure of anything, do not install. Error on the side of caution

- ✓ If a software publisher asks for a small donation, consider it. It costs money to produce good quality software. If you want to see more product from them, donate. A small donation is cheaper than commercial alternatives

CHAPTER FOURTEEN

EPILOGUE

FINAL THOUGHTS

Learning is a continual and lifelong journey. Never stop! Explore new, different, alternative and strange. Some people thought Edison was a fool when time after time an experiment did not work as he intended, but Edison was not discouraged. He saw each failed attempt as a step forward. Life is like that. Forward momentum is always better than being paralyzed or crippled by fear and indecision. In this book forward movement and learning is encouraged throughout its pages. Anything better does not come about by accident. Most people like what is familiar and the same. Change is hard, but not impossible.

The author and publisher of this book hope that you have discovered something new – something you want to try. While every attempt has been made to ensure accuracy, the author and publisher is not liable for negative consequences that result from the use of the information provided. Omissions are accidental and, arise because of the ever-changing technology landscape.

If you find any of this information useful, please consider recommending this book to others or share some the ideas that you found inside it.

Thank you for the time you took to read this book. Please look for future publications from Serendipitous Finds. You can find more information at

http://www.positiveperspectives.online

www.serendipitousfinds.online

SOURCES AND REFERENCES

The author of this book would like to acknowledge, credit and thank

the following for their content used within its pages

These Sources and corresponding URL's are acknowledged within the

footnotes of this book and listed again here. They provide additional

information and sources of further study and greater detail.

Bibliography

"Adobe: Creative, Marketing and Document Management Solutions." Adobe: Creative, marketing and document management solutions. Accessed June 7, 2019. https://www.adobe.com/ca/.

"Apache OpenOffice - Official Site - The Free and Open Productivity Suite." Accessed June 7, 2019. http://www.openoffice.org/.

content, Tim Fisher Tim Fisher has 30+ years' professional technology support experience He writes troubleshooting, and is the General Manager of Lifewire. "How to Erase a Hard Drive Using DBAN." Lifewire. Accessed June 7, 2019. https://www.lifewire.com/how-to-erase-a-hard-drive-using-dban-2619148.

"DistroWatch.Com: Put the Fun Back into Computing. Use Linux, BSD." Accessed June 7, 2019. https://distrowatch.com/.

"Google Photos - All Your Photos Organized and Easy to Find." Accessed June 7, 2019. https://www.google.com/photos/about/.

"Honey." Honey. Accessed June 7, 2019. https://www.joinhoney.com/feed.

March 6, Conner Forrest in Software on, 2019, and 9:19 Am Pst. "20 Apple Keyboard Shortcuts Business Users Need to Know." TechRepublic. Accessed June 7, 2019. https://www.techrepublic.com/article/20-apple-keyboard-shortcuts-business-users-need-to-know/.

"News | Open Source Initiative." Accessed June 7, 2019. https://opensource.org/.

"RetailMeNot: Coupons, Cash Back, Gift Card Deals, Genie & More." RetailMeNot.com. Accessed June 7, 2019. https://www.retailmenot.com/.

Rhee, Ed. "How to Securely Erase an SSD Drive." CNET. Accessed June 7, 2019. https://www.cnet.com/how-to/how-to-securely-erase-an-ssd-drive/.

"SmugMug: Protect, Share, Store, and Sell Your Photos." Accessed June 7, 2019. https://www.smugmug.com/.

"Top 9 Apps to Batch Install & Uninstall Windows Apps." Hongkiat, January 25, 2016. https://www.hongkiat.com/blog/batch-install-uninstall-windows/.

"Urban Dictionary: Leadite." Urban Dictionary. Accessed June 7, 2019. https://www.urbandictionary.com/define.php?term=Leadite.

Warren, Tom. "The Best Windows 10 Keyboard Shortcuts." The Verge, July 29, 2015. https://www.theverge.com/2015/7/29/9065973/microsoft-windows-10-keyboard-shortcuts-list.

"What You Need to Know About Creating System Image Backups." Accessed June 7, 2019. https://www.howtogeek.com/192115/what-you-need-to-know-about-creating-system-image-backups/.

ENDNOTES

[1] "20 Apple Shortcuts Business Users Need to Know", Conner Forrest
https://www.techrepublic.com/article/20-apple-keyboard-shortcuts-business-users-need-to-know/ , March 6, 2019.

[2] "The Best Windows 10 Keyboard Shortcuts", Tom Warren,
https://www.theverge.com/2015/7/29/9065973/microsoft-windows-10-keyboard-shortcuts-list, July 29, 2015

[3]
https://en.wikipedia.org/wiki/Health_Insurance_Portability_and_Accountability_Act

[4]"How to erase a Hard Drive Using DBAN", Tim Fisher,
https://www.cnet.com/how-to/how-to-securely-erase-an-ssd-drive/ May 13, 2019.

[5] How to Securely Erase an SSD Drive", Ed Rhee,
https://www.cnet.com/how-to/how-to-securely-erase-an-ssd-drive/
October 5, 2011

[6] "Windows Lifecycle Fact Sheep", Microsoft,
https://support.microsoft.com/en-ca/help/13853/windows-lifecycle-fact-sheet June 2019

[7] "Top 10 Apps to Batch Install & Uninstall Widows Apps", Ashutosh KS,

Hongkiat, "https://www.hongkiat.com/blog/batch-install-uninstall-windows/ October 14, 2017

www.ingramcontent.com/pod-product-compliance
Lightning Source LLC
Chambersburg PA
CBHW031223050326
40689CB00009B/1446